# Reconstruction

**The word is woven**

**Into our everyday lives**

**Angie Hulsey**

All Scripture quotations are taken from the Kings James Version of the Bible.

Reconstruction
The word is woven
Into our everyday lives

ISBN 979-8-9942917-0-2 (paperback)
Front cover design by Brittany Hulsey

Published by Angie Hulsey, Bonne Terre, MO

# Gratitude

Above everything, I give thanks to God. This book exists only because He spoke to me, directed my path, corrected my course, and carried me through. His voice calmed me, His presence empowers me, and it was His grace that made the impossible possible. God is the Author of my story and the Guardian of my soul, transforming every struggle I faced into testimony. To Him belongs all the glory.

To my parents, I am grateful for your unwavering faith, constant prayers, and the solid foundation you established long before I recognised its value. Your commitment to God, your resilience, and your love shaped who I am today. The seeds you sowed are now bearing fruit in my life, and through my children, your legacy continues. I sincerely appreciate the inheritance you preserved and entrusted to me.

To my husband, thank you for walking beside me through seasons that were heavy, strange, stretching, and holy. Thank you for your patience, your support, and your willingness to stand with me even when you didn't fully see what God was showing me. Your presence has been a steady place for my heart, and I am grateful for the life we are building together.

To my four children-each, each of you is a miracle, a promise, and a reminder of God's faithfulness. You are the joy that keeps me going and the reason I fight with such determination. Your lives carry purpose, calling, and heaven's fingerprints. Thank you for your love, your laughter, and the way you pull me closer to God simply by being

To everyone who reads this book, thank you. My prayer is that the same God who met me will meet you, speak to you, and strengthen you in ways that change your life forever.

## Authors note

Everything in this book is my personal testimony: my experiences, my encounters, and the moments when God met me in ways I never expected. I am not teaching doctrine or asking anyone to build their beliefs on my story. I am simply sharing what I lived, what I saw, and what God walked me through.

My prayer is that my journey points you back to Jesus and encourages you to seek Him for yourself. Scripture remains the final authority, and nothing I share replaces God's Word. I submit every experience with humility and toward Him.

I am a witness to His power, not a teacher of doctrine. These pages are my testimony, offered in obedience and with a grateful heart.

# The Early Threads

My life started in a spiritual battle. Two months before I was conceived, my mom was in a waiting room waiting to be called for a tubal ligation. My mom said a voice in her head told her to leave. So she did. The lord had his hand on me before he even formed me.

**Jeremiah 1:5**
Before I formed you in the womb, I knew you; Before you were born, I sanctified you;
I ordained you a prophet to the nations.

Growing up, my memories are painted with both bright and dark moments. I was drawn to the words in red—even before I could read, I wanted to look at them. Singing to Him brought me joy, and "All the Little Children" was always my favourite song.

Yet, darkness crept in; early nights were tough. Sometimes I saw a shadowy figure standing at the foot of my bed. Other times, I would dream of trying to cast demons out of people, but in those dreams, the demon always laughed, and I could never banish it.

As I grew older and was filled with the Holy Spirit, everything changed. I had one final dream about casting out a demon; this time, the demon didn't laugh. In that dream, it left the woman and sat beside her on the ground. I was about to stop praying when I heard a voice say, "Don't stop." So I continued praying, and the demon fell through the floor and disappeared. I understood then that she was finally free.

Looking back, I realise those unsettling dreams were actually a gift from God. He was training me, even from my earliest days.

# Roots of faith

From a young age, I saw things I wished I hadn't. There were nights when fear sent me running to my parents' room, and other times I was too afraid to move—so I hid under my covers and prayed. My mom always knew what to do. She'd tell me: Plead the blood of Jesus over what you see. If it's evil, it will leave. If it remains, it's from God.

She taught me to do this every time, reminding me that the devil is a liar and often pretends to be of God. It was clear—always test every spirit. Now, as an adult, this practice has become second nature, even shaping my dreams. Teaching your children to discern and test the spirits is essential.

**1 Peter 5:8**

Be sober, be vigilant; because your adversary the devil walks about like a roaring lion, seeking whom he may devour.

## When I turned away

Then came my teenage years, and they drew me away from Him. I no longer made time for God. The dreams stopped, but the dark figure would still show up, almost like clockwork— about once every six months. I would try to handle it on my own for a few nights, but when it became overwhelming, I would finally tell my mom. She would pray, and then the darkness would disappear for another six months, continuing this cycle until she passed away.

Strangely, it never occurred to me that I could pray about it myself. I remember wondering what would happen after my mom was gone and assuming the darkness would come every night for the rest of my life. It's odd to think I never realised I could pray, but that was my reality then. How is that possible?

I now understand this was a monitoring demon assigned to watch and wait for me to step into my calling God had for me.

## John 12:40

He has blinded their eyes and hardened their hearts, lest they should see with their eyes, lest they should understand with their hearts and turn, so that I should heal them.

# The Day My Faith Shattered

When I was 25, my father was diagnosed with cancer. I truly believed God would heal him. My dad's faith is in loving the Lord completely. I couldn't imagine God allowing someone like him to endure such a painful end. The week leading up to his death was the longest of my life—filled with indescribable pain and overwhelming anger toward God. How could a loving God let this happen to someone so faithful? Each day, my anger grew. Watching my father suffer

My anger pushed God out of my heart completely. At that point, it was as if God no longer existed for me. He wouldn't come back to my mind until much later, when I finally called out to Him. After I was saved, God gave me my first vision. I was at my kitchen table when I suddenly felt as though I was lifted, looking through someone else's eyes. In that moment, I saw that God hadn't done anything cruel to my father—He had given him the most beautiful gift. I saw all six of us, my siblings and

I, gathered around my father's deathbed, witnessing his pain yet also watching him declare his trust and love for God.

In that vision, I saw seeds being sown into each of us, and hooks placed in our jaws—the Lord's promise that He would pursue all my father's children with relentless love. I realised then that this was God's final gift to my dad, a blessing that would follow us for the rest of our lives. When my time comes, I can only hope to be as blessed.

**Ezekiel 29:4**

But I will put hooks in your jaws, and cause the fish of your rivers to stick to your scales; I will bring you up out of the midst of your rivers, and all the fish in your rivers will stick to your scales;

**John 12:24**

Most assuredly, I say to you, unless a grain of wheat falls into the ground and dies, it remains alone, but if it dies, it produces much grain.

# When the unseen sat beside me

The week after my father passed, my spiritual senses seemed to heighten. I began to see things in the spirit again. At night, I would wake and see my dad sitting at the foot of my bed—healthy, smiling, and peaceful. He never spoke; he would just look at me, and then he would vanish. Sometimes, after a shower, I would find his name—Tom—written in the fog on the bathroom mirror, the only word he could spell. The TV would turn on by itself. Strange as it was, these experiences gave me comfort. I was sure my dad loved us so much that he had stayed to protect us, to watch over us.

My oldest son, Dylan, was six at the time. One day, his school called to say they were concerned; at recess, he would stand under the tree where my dad used to pick him up after school. Dylan claimed to have seen my dad there, too. In my grief, I convinced myself this was a blessing—that my dad was still with us, safeguarding his family. It's easy to see, now, how the enemy works: using our deepest pains, our love and longing, to deceive us.

I wanted to talk to my mom about it; I knew what she would say. She would pray, and things would change. Deep down, I sensed something was off. Even though I believed in almost everything about the afterlife except what the Bible says, I somehow knew this wasn't really my dad.

Some weeks later, while at my mom's house, she asked if I had seen my dad. She told me he had visited her twice, and both times she rebuked him. She said that the last time, the spirit told her, "If you make me leave, I can't come back." My mom said, "Angie, that's not your dad, and you know it—it's a familiar spirit." After her prayer, all the strange happenings stopped.

My mother had an unshakable faith. She could simply pray from her chair, and things, no matter how far away, would shift. I always wondered how she had such spiritual authority. After I surrendered my life to Christ, God blessed me with a heart to intercede for others as my mother did.

**Romans 8:26-27**

26 Likewise the spirit also helps in our weakness. For we do not know what we should pray for us we ought, but the spirit Himself makes intercession for us with groaning which cannot be uttered.

27 Now He who searches the hearts knows what the mind of the Spirit is, because He makes intercession for the saints according to the will of God.

# Living Water

A week after I stopped seeing my dad, I had the most vivid dream. It's been over two decades, but I remember every detail as if it happened last night. In my dream, my dad stood in the middle of an endless field. He looked incredible—healthy again, absolutely glowing. The grass around him was tall and brilliant with colour. There was a single, massive tree in the centre, towering above everything.

My dad began running through the field, motioning for me to follow. I tried to keep up, feeling his excitement as we moved together. We finally reached a stream, more beautiful than anything I've ever seen. The water sparkled with such clarity that I could see every colourful stone shining beneath its surface. My dad knelt, dipped his hand into the stream, and brought the water to his lips, a broad smile on his face. "Angie, all you have to do is drink it," he said, laughing. "That's all you have to do."

That dream never left me. Sometimes, I think about the contrast: the memory of my dad passing, and this image of him in the field, filled with life and joy, urging me towards the water. It made me question—why was my dad so thrilled about this water? Why did he want me to drink it so badly?

It wasn't until after I was saved that I truly understood: God was personally inviting me to the Living Water. The enemy will try every trick to distract us, even using people and memories we love. He can only imitate; he can never create. He might offer something that looks amazing, but it's not the real thing. That's why we have to be careful—listen for God's voice above everything else. God's plans are far greater, more beautiful than we could ever imagine. His invitation is always real: Just come and drink. His water bring life.

**John 4:13-14**

13 Jesus answered and said to her, "Whoever drinks of this water will thirst again.

14 but whoever drinks of the water that I shall give him will never thirst. But the water that I shall give him will become in him a fountain of water, springing up into everlasting.

# My testimony

After my mother passed away, I was swept up in a storm of emotions. At that point in my life, I wasn't saved. I held a thousand different beliefs about the afterlife, yet somehow, deep down, I knew she was in heaven. I missed her deeply, of course, but mixed with my sadness was a strange excitement for her— she had finally reached the place she always longed to be.

Despite this, fear crept into my heart. I found myself on edge, waiting for the return of the dark, hooded figure from my nightmares. What would I do now, without my mom's prayers to protect me? Six months went by—nothing. Nearly a year— still nothing. I began to wonder if this presence was somehow tied to my mother. Was it gone for good?

Then, just a week before the anniversary of my mom's passing, everything changed. My youngest child started to talk about God and asked, "Why don't we go to church?" I was surprised—where were these questions coming from? That same week, the dreams began again. These were the most tormenting dreams I'd ever had—dark, oppressive, and twisted. It wasn't just the images; it was the feeling in the dreams, so real it clung to me even after I woke. I would see myself sitting and talking to my mom, only to feel my skin crawl, as if it had been turned inside out. The sense of evil was overwhelming, worse than anything I had ever experienced. Each night, the dreams grew more intense. My mom's image would say horrible things about God—telling me that God was torturing my dad, casting doubt and pain into my heart.

Would be saying horrible things about God. It would tell me God was torturing my dad. In my dreams, I would say, "You're not my mom," and she would turn into a minor black demon and scream, "No." That God wouldn't let them be together. The dream that changed my life was the one in which I called my mom a liar. She was telling me God is nothing but a liar. In that moment, something inside of me came alive. Like nothing I've ever felt. Something deep down inside of me came up. I stood up, looked at my mom, and said, "No, you're the liar." In that moment, everything inside me broke. Like I just busted out of a room I've been a prisoner in my whole life. In that moment, I truly grasped and felt my love for God. I stood boldly, ready to defend Him. Suddenly, my mother's image transformed into a minor, black demon, shrieking "No, no, no," and shaking its head with violent fury. I could sense the deep hatred it had for me. It was then I understood—the enemy had specifically targeted me. God allowed the test: "If you can deceive her using her mother's face…" But the enemy underestimated the power of a mother's influence on her child.

That realisation changed everything. I knew I couldn't let the enemy use my image in the same way; I resolved to ensure my children would see God in me. Right then and there, I asked God to change me, to claim my life as His own, and I committed to doing everything possible to protect my family.

The last dream I had about my mom was vivid: I stood in my kitchen, and as she entered, a strong sense of evil washed over me—more intense than ever before. Oddly enough, I wasn't afraid; I was angry that the devil would use my mother's likeness. I knew she wouldn't have wanted that. In the dream, I was washing dishes when I turned around and saw her; I threw the dish, shattering it. Pointing at her, I declared, "That's it, I'm calling Aunt Sue." After my parents passed, Aunt Sue was the only Christian I truly trusted. I knew she loved the Lord.

Instantly, my mom's image reverted to the demon. It raced across the room so quickly—it didn't run, just suddenly appeared nose to nose with me, screaming, "NO!"

The next morning, I tried to call Aunt Sue, but her number had mysteriously vanished from my phone—though I'd had it memorised for years. It took me a week to reach her, and by then, the dreams had stopped. When I finally explained everything, including how I threatened the demon with her name, she understood. She told me that the same week, she'd experienced a nightmare so dark she knew it was from the devil. She awoke, rebuked it in prayer, and the oppression was broken. The demon had gone to test her authority in Christ—and found it greater than its own. That experience taught me the importance of surrounding yourself with people of strong faith.

### Luke 22:31-32

31 And the Lord said "Simon, Simon! Indeed, Satan has asked for you, that he may sift you as wheat. 32 But I have prayed for you, that your faith should not fail; and when you have returned to Me, strengthen your brethren."

### 2 Chronicles 7:14

If my people who are called by My name will humble themselves, and pray and seek my face, and turn from their wicked ways, then I will hear from heaven, and will forgive their sins and heal their land.

# Reconstruction Begins

Now, the Lord began to lift the blindfold from my eyes—and I am incredibly grateful He did so gently. From my perspective, life seemed okay. I thought there were no real issues. Even now, I can hardly comprehend how blind I was. My husband was a functional alcoholic, but that didn't faze me. As long as he was working, paying bills, and we got our vacations (which I thought was most important), I ignored the rest.

Meanwhile, beneath the surface, my family was hurting. One of my sons struggled with a spirit of suicide that would occasionally rear its head. My beautiful daughter was battling self-harm, and I had absolutely no idea. I'm her mother—how could I have missed the signs? My other son has severe autism and is nonverbal, while yet another son had significant behavioural challenges. I had my own faults too—especially my words and the way I sometimes treated people. Looking back, I realise I either couldn't see these issues or refused to face them.

Right after I was saved, my husband spiralled—from a functional alcoholic to barely functioning at all. Suddenly, my family felt utterly shattered, broken into countless pieces in countless ways. I remember being in the shower, praying—a total breakdown moment. I pleaded with God to help us, not to let the enemy destroy my children. I cried out for a miracle to save them.

As I prayed, God gave me a vision of a tent pole breaking apart, falling to pieces because the strings holding it together had snapped. There were six pieces—the same number as our family. Then God spoke to my heart: "If you stop what you're doing and follow Me, I'll make your family so strong that nothing will ever break you again." In an instant, that fragile, broken pole became a thick, solid rod.

A deep peace came over me. My tears dried up, and an unexplainable strength filled me. I stood taller—with a boldness grounded in God's promise: my family would not die but live to declare His works to the nations.

In that moment, I promised God my life—fully and completely—trusting Him to do whatever He desired with me. My life is no longer my own. I have been bought with a price, covered by His blood, and my faith is forever anchored in Him.

### John 12:40

"He has blinded their eyes and hardened their hearts, Lest they should see with their eyes, Lest they should understand with their hearts and turn, So that I should heal them."

# Light reveals what was hidden.

I wasn't saved in a church; instead, God met me in a dream. The week following that experience was eye-opening, to say the least. Suddenly, my spiritual eyes were open. I began seeing demons—mostly at night. They would walk around, silently watching me. It was terrifying; I remember a lot of screaming and many nights spent sleeping with the lights on.

It struck me as strange: when I served the devil, I only ever saw one black-hooded figure. Now that I was serving God, I was seeing demons everywhere. I realised they had been around me all my life—I just hadn't been able to see them until the Light showed up.

I thought of how my mom had always known how to fight these things. I felt excited because I thought I knew what to do too: I would find a church, tell them about what I was experiencing, and get the help I needed. I believed it would finally be over.

But when I sought help from the Pentecostal church I visited, I was met not with support but with judgment. People told me, "That's not of God," or "If you stop giving them attention, they'll leave. The devil is just messing with you." I was desperate, telling anyone who would listen about my struggles with demons. Before long, I became known as the lady at church obsessed with demons—always full of zeal, always talking about spiritual things. But the truth was, I just wanted someone to help me.

I asked so many Christians about demons—at least a hundred people—and I couldn't believe that none of them saw what I was seeing. It made me question if something was wrong with me. How could these believers be so unaware? At the time, I was new to church life and didn't understand that we all have different gifts. I simply didn't know about the gift of spiritual discernment.

At a Tuesday night prayer meeting, I shared again about a recent experience: waking up to see a demon sniffing my husband as he slept. The looks I received told me how unusual my story sounded. Afterwards, a kind woman approached me. She said, "When you were speaking, I knew you had a discerning spirit." I had never heard that term before and asked her what it meant. She explained that I was sensitive to the spiritual realm. Her words were an answer to prayer—I finally understood why I was different. She treated me with kindness and understanding; to this day, I admire her for it.

Around this same time, God sent me the community I had been longing for—a group of friends who experienced the spiritual world as I did. It was a tremendous relief, and these friends have become some of the most important people in my life.

They discipled me, and I began to realise that it was God allowing me to see these things. The devil wants to hide, and God was showing me where to pray and what to pray against. He had been training me my whole life, preparing me to stand in spiritual battle. I learned how to cast out demons, not because it was entertaining, but because it was necessary for the calling on my life.

If you see into the spirit, it's for a reason—don't let anyone convince you otherwise. The Holy Spirit will lift you, but the accuser will try to tear you down. Be careful who you share your experiences with; some people will misunderstand, judge, or label you. I even became friends with a pastor—Pastor

Allen—and his wonderful wife. They welcomed me into their Friday night meetings at their home, where my new circle would gather. We learned, worshipped, and invited the Holy Spirit to move. Those were powerful nights.

Today, I walk in new boldness and am growing in the Lord. The Word is alive in me. I am no longer afraid or screaming when I see demons. I now fight with heaven's backing, not in my own strength—and the demons have begun to keep their distance. They no longer come inside my bedroom. Now, they stand at the door, and the moment I start praying, they leave.

### Matthew 7:6
"Do not give what is holy to the dogs; nor cast your pearls before swine, lest they trample them under their feet, and turn and tear you in pieces.

### Ephesians 6:11
Put on the whole armor of God, that you may be able to stand against the wiles of the devil.

### Luke 15:4

"What man of you, having a hundred sheep, if he loses one of them, does not leave the ninety-nine in the wilderness, and go after the one which is lost until he finds it?

# When God Became My Teacher

The first year after I was saved was a year of intense spiritual warfare—not by choice. There was no gentle transition for me, from darkness to light; instead, it was as if I was thrust straight into the battle. I didn't just get to say a cute, simple prayer and move forward. Instead, I would be jolted awake at night, confronted by terrifying, demonic images and presences. Each time, it truly felt like a fight. I would pray with everything in me, declaring the authority of Jesus, commanding every evil thing to leave in His name, insisting they had no right to me or my home.

To this day, that's how I pray—with boldness, declaring God's power and authority over every situation, knowing the enemy has no dominion. Over that long and challenging year, I learned an invaluable lesson: the very act of seeing these things wasn't the enemy's doing—it was God. He was with me through every frightening moment, watching, guiding, and teaching me to stand firm in the authority He's given me. He used those nights of warfare to help me grow in faith and in prayer.

I was no longer alone; God sent friends to disciple and encourage me. I noticed that when I prayed, things shifted in the spiritual realm—still most often at night. Sometimes, I'd wake and see a demon at the foot of my bed. I would pray, "I plead the blood of Jesus over you." I remember watching a single raindrop fall onto its head, turning it to smoke, and the demon would vanish. Once, black fog crept under my bedroom door. Again, I pleaded the blood, and a striking electric-red light covered it, dissolving it instantly.

Not every encounter was with darkness. On some nights, I'd see a beautiful, electric-red light flowing like a river across my ceiling. I've even seen angels in my house. I often wondered— why did I see more demons than angels? But in my heart, I knew there were always more angels surrounding my family than demons. I didn't have to see them to trust that they were fighting with me.

One night, I woke and saw a little girl standing outside my bedroom door. As before, I pleaded the blood of Jesus over her. Usually, these spirits vanished instantly, but this time, a radiant angel appeared next to her. The angel raised her hand toward the girl, who disappeared. This angel was as tall as my door, with braided hair, a beautiful cross necklace, and wings wrapped around her—all shimmering, pure white.

God showed me through these experiences that it isn't my words themselves that hold power, but rather that my words activate help from heaven. My words are a call for God's intervention. The demon didn't flee because I said, "I plead the blood of Jesus"—it left because the angel, responding to my faith, commanded it to go.

During all those encounters, I was only touched by a demon once. I was lying in bed when I felt something grab my wrist. I looked—and saw what looked almost comical: a black sheet with holes cut for eyes. I didn't even have time to pray when a bright blue light began radiating from its eyes, and it darted around the room with supernatural speed, as if it was desperate to escape something I couldn't see. Later, my friends explained that when an angel and a demon clash, a blue light often accompanies their conflict. That knowledge lifted my trust in the Lord to a whole new level—I knew my angel was in my room, protecting me, even as I was about to fall asleep, not praying, worshipping, or reading Scripture. God's promise of protection is so faithful and honest.

After nearly a year, the demonic activity began to fade, until I stopped seeing them altogether—unless God revealed one so I would know what to pray for in someone's life. I believe He let me go through that season to reveal the reality of the spiritual realm—to strengthen my faith and equip me for the calling He placed on my life.

I'm grateful that season is behind me—but, if God asked, I would walk through it again. Through it all, He truly became my Teacher, my Defender, and the One I trust beyond all else.

**Deuteronomy 32:2**

Let my teaching drop as the rain, My speech distill as the drew,
As raindrops on the tender herb, And as showers on the grass.

## Zechariah 2:5

For I, says the Lord, "will be a wall of fire all around her, and I will be the glory in her midst.:

## Luke 10:19

Behold, I give you authority to trample on serpents and scorpions, and over all the powers of the enemy, and nothing shall by any means hurt you.

# When the spirit filled me, Darkness reacted.

About six months after I was saved, I was filled with the Holy Spirit—an experience made even more special because it happened to my sister and me on the same day. I will never forget every detail of that moment. I was at a new church, a place I had only visited a couple of times before. It was a large congregation, one where the Holy Spirit's presence seemed to be welcome and active.

During worship, I felt called to the altar. The Holy Spirit was moving, baptising people in the Spirit. I had tried to experience this before, but each attempt left me feeling discouraged, like it just wasn't for me. I went forward with lingering doubts, already convinced nothing would happen—a lie I now recognise as the whisper of the enemy.

The pastor's wife began praying for me to be filled. At first, nothing changed. After a while, I told her it was okay if we stopped. She shook her head and said, "No, I feel it right here— it's waiting on something." She gently asked, "Is there anything

God has done for you that you haven't thanked Him for?" Immediately, I thought of my mom's dream. I was overwhelmed—tears poured out as I began to thank God for rescuing me from that darkness.

The moment I offered my gratitude, something incredible happened. I could suddenly sense my body in one place, while my soul felt far away. I wasn't afraid. Everything was black, but I could hear myself—just as in my mom's dream—crying out desperately for Jesus. That's when God showed me the moment I first called out to Him: the instant I cried out, He was already there, waiting for me.

When I came back to myself, a stream of unfamiliar words poured from my mouth. I looked at the pastor's wife and asked, "Did it happen?" She smiled, saying, "Oh, it happened." I remember the salty taste lingering on my lips for days.

After church, I returned home. At this time, my husband was still struggling with alcoholism. As soon as I walked in the door, he looked at me and growled—an animalistic sound he made several more times that day. At first, I thought he was joking, but when I asked why, he seemed genuinely confused; he didn't remember doing it. I didn't understand then, but quickly learned that demons do not like someone filled with the Holy Spirit.

In the months that followed, I began to notice others growling as they passed me. In public, people I didn't know would growl. Even at church, some would hiss. I hadn't yet found my circle of spiritually gifted friends, so I was left baffled. I asked fellow church members why this was happening, but I was only met with puzzled or uncomfortable looks.

Finding my circle brought enormous relief. I wasn't alone or crazy—some people are simply called more strongly to deliverance. But through all this, God taught me an important lesson: don't let your whole life revolve around the enemy's activity. One morning in my kitchen, the Lord asked me, "What will you say on judgment day if I ask: 'You knew all about My deliverance ministry, but that's all you knew about Me'? You might find you never really knew me at all."

I wept with conviction and repented. My deepest desire became to know God fully and intimately. When my time on earth ends, I want to step into heaven feeling no separation between my life here and my life with Him. The devil will always try to pull our focus into constant warfare, keeping us engaged with him instead of with God. Don't let the battle consume your attention; remember to seek balance and keep your heart, above all, set on knowing the Lord.

### Acts 1:5

For John truly baptised with water, but you shall be baptised with the Holy Spirit, not many days from now.

### Colossians 4:6

Let your speech always be with grace, seasoned with salt, that you may know how you ought to answer each one.

### Matthew 10:1

And when He had called His twelve disciples to Him, He gave them power over unclean spirits, to cast them out, and to heal all kinds of sickness and all kinds of diseases.

# Unforgiven has to go.

The first year after I was saved, things quickly took a turn for the worse. Up until then, my husband was a functional alcoholic. But the minute God entered my life, he could no longer function at all. Now I understand—it was because light had entered our darkness, and the enemy didn't like it one bit. When God stepped in, our lives hit rock bottom. I couldn't comprehend it at the time, but now I know: God, as a good Father, needed to show us that our behaviour would destroy us. He doesn't enable His children—He corrects us, even when it hurts.

God started working on my husband, but it was a spiritual battle. Hell was not going to let him go easily. As God drew my husband, his condition seemed to worsen. I want to be clear— my husband was never mean to our children or me; he was simply absent, checked out, in no way involved in family life. That caused a lot of pain. Watching him fall apart felt almost unbearable; it seemed hopeless. But in the spirit realm, God had begun a battle for our family. He called my husband's name, and the enemy fought back. My husband had to be broken so God could rebuild him.

It was the most challenging year of my life. I began seeing demons, while everyone around me insisted I was just imagining things. My husband was in no shape to help—I felt utterly alone and thought maybe I was losing my mind.

A couple of months before my husband's breakthrough, I hit the wall emotionally. I finally admitted: I couldn't carry this pain anymore. I didn't want to keep living with this hurt. I prayed and prayed, desperate for relief. I couldn't let it go, no matter how hard I tried.

One night at church, my pastor issued an altar call for those struggling with unforgiveness. If you needed to forgive but didn't know how, you were invited to come forward. So I did. There was a line of people. When my pastor reached me, he placed his hand on my head and declared, "She forgave—come off her now." Instantly, I felt a supernatural weight lift from my shoulders, as if someone had physically picked me up from the ground. I'd never felt anything like it.

But I realised there were still two people I hadn't forgiven. I had nursed anger toward them for a long time, though I couldn't fully understand why. It was my secret—no one, not even my husband, knew how I felt. After the prayer, I wondered why I was free from my husband's weight, but not from these two. On the way home, I knew I needed to confess my feelings.

That night, I sat down beside my husband—who, thankfully, was doing better than usual—and shared my heart. I explained everything to him. He surprised me by saying he understood and could see why I felt that way. The moment I stood up, I suddenly realised the weight was gone from me. I spent the next few days in awe of how light I felt, amazed at how easy it was to walk simply.

I couldn't pray away the burden I felt for my husband, because it had to be commanded to go. But with those two people, healing only came when I confessed my sin. Then, freedom followed. Yes, unforgiveness is a sin, a legal right for the enemy. Through all of this, I believe God was also showing me how much I needed my husband—and how much I needed honest communication and confession. It felt so good to talk to him. I truly needed that connection.

## Matthew 6:14-15

14"For if you forgive men their trespasses, your heavenly Father will also forgive you. 15 But if you do not forgive men their trespasses, neither will your Father forgive your trespasses.

## 1 John 1:9

If we confess our sins, He is faithful and just to forgive us our sins and to cleanse us from all unrighteousness

# My first deliverance was myself.

The first deliverance I ever experienced was of myself. I had already been saved for a while, and I was filled with the Holy Spirit. I realise that's a debated topic for some, but this is my story—no one can tell me what God has or hasn't done in my life. God was changing me day by day, yet I still faced one major struggle I couldn't seem to overcome: I was plagued by intrusive, perverse thoughts. I never knew when they were coming or how long they'd last. Sometimes, I would just be sitting at the kitchen table when they would appear, and I knew deep down it was more than just my own mind. I didn't want these thoughts and couldn't control them.

I began praying, asking God to show me the root of the problem and why I was having these thoughts. The very next day, when the house was empty, I searched YouTube for deliverance from perverted thoughts. What I discovered was both frightening and eye-opening, making me realise just how real the spiritual realm truly is. I found a video about casting out a spirit called Lilith. When I saw the image, I was shocked—it was the same demon I saw in my mom's dreams. I wondered, How long has this spirit been part of my life?

I watched the entire deliverance video, following along with prayers of renunciation, breaking soul ties, and declaring freedom. All at once, I felt a powerful sensation—a heavy seed shot up through my throat with such force that it stunned me. I went to spit it out, but nothing came out. Still, I knew something had left me. I immediately thanked God for His deliverance.

From that moment on, the perverse thoughts stopped entirely. Not a single one returned. If you find yourself unable to control your thoughts, know that there might be a deeper issue at work. Seek the Lord—those thoughts of suicide, murder, or self-harm are not from God. Take every thought captive, and trust that God truly can set you free.

**2 Timothy 4:18**

And the lord will deliver me from every evil work and preserve me for His heavenly kingdom. To Him be glory forever and ever. Amen;

**2 Corinthians 10:5**

Casting down arguments and every high thing that exalts itself against the knowledge of God, bring every thought into captivity to the obedience of christ.

# Chains Broken

About six months after I was filled with the Holy Spirit, I chose to go through deliverance. At that point, I was immersed in Scripture, prayer, and daily worship. By all appearances, I was living as the Bible teaches—but I still struggled with certain things Christians suddent face. Honestly, I don't know if a demon can literally be inside you or not, and I don't think it matters. All deliverance is, at its heart, prayer. The only painful part of deliverance is letting go of things we've grown used to. My testimony is my own experience—others may have different stories.

I went through my session with two friends, Dani and Nikki. It lasted about three hours, and for the first two, we simply prayed and asked the Holy Spirit to reveal any legal rights that might be holding me back. There was an invisible wall we couldn't break. I renounced everything I could think of, but the blockage remained. Eventually, the Holy Spirit kept showing us it was about blood. Without Him guiding us, I would have never seen it. Demons can bury things so deep you only uncover them through prayer.

After a while, another piece of the puzzle surfaced. My mom had passed away almost a year and a half before, and the moment I was saved, I became convinced it was up to me to get my four brothers saved, too, as if their eternity depended on me. The Holy Spirit showed me I was angry at my mom for leaving us. I broke down and wept, finally saying, "Mom, I forgive you for leaving me." At that moment, with tears running down my face, I felt the wall shatter into a million pieces.

Dani said she saw me chained to a concrete wall, held by six massive chains. She described the pressure I felt—trying to pray my family into heaven, believing it all depended on me. The enemy had me so busy and consumed with this burden that I couldn't focus on anything else. That kind of pressure is bondage. God would never put that on us. My friends declared each chain broken in Jesus' name and rebuked the devil's lies, setting me free. From that day, I was able to pray with absolute peace, focusing on what God wanted.

During the session, we came across a Python spirit. It was unsettling; I literally felt a snake move out from the top of my head. I'd always had a severe fear of snakes—I couldn't even look at them on TV. But a week later, in the park with my kids, I spotted a giant black snake. Usually, I would have run away screaming. This time, I simply watched, feeling nothing at all. It showed me that real deliverance changes you.

We called out many spirits that day, and as each one left, it was as if I saw my friends differently through new eyes—as the spiritual world shifted. Even during the process, thoughts popped into my head, like the urge to kick my friend, but I immediately rejected them. In the days that followed, my mind felt strangely quiet, free from clutter and noise—a completely new experience.

The most significant change came in worship. Before, my thoughts would always drift or turn into strange prayers for others when I tried to sing. Now, I could worship and focus entirely on the Lord. My mind was finally free. Demons don't care if you pray—worship is what torments them. If you find yourself praying every time you try to worship, something deeper may need to be addressed.

Whether the spirits were "inside" my body or not, I can't say for sure. After this session, I was free. God began moving in my family like never before; I could hear Him so clearly, and peace rushed in. I believe everyone should seek deliverance—at its core, it's just prayer.

One thing that stands out is how divided people get over the question of whether a Spirit-filled Christian can have a demon. Both sides seem determined to prove they're right, fighting while the devil just watches. The truth is, we're on the same side. It shouldn't matter where the demon is; what matters is breaking the power of the enemy and standing united. A house divided can't stand. We know the enemy exists—so command it to leave in Jesus' name and let's get in agreement, putting aside petty arguments to advance the Kingdom.

### Ephesians 2:14

For He Himself is our peace, who has made both one, and has broken down the middle wall of separation.

## Psalm 107:14

He brought them out of darkness and the shadow of death, And broke their chains in pieces.

## 2 Corinthians 10:5

Casting down arguments and every high thing that exalts itself against the knowledge of God, bring every thought into captivity to the obedience of christ.

## 2 Timothy 4:18

And the lord will deliver me from every evil work and preserve me for His heavenly kingdom. To Him be glory forever and ever. Amen

# Life after Deliverance

Since my deliverance, I've been able to hear God's voice more clearly than ever before. There was one morning at church that especially showed me how real this is. Typically, I go to the altar during worship, but that morning, for reasons I couldn't explain, I stayed in my seat.

As worship began, I had a clear view of Mariah, a newer girl at church whom I'd first met at a tent revival a few weeks prior. Mariah was praying between two women: my pastor's wife and a powerful, anointed woman named Alicia.

As I watched, I sensed the Lord urging me to go to Mariah and share a Bible verse with her. Doubt flooded my mind—who was I to step in? The verse itself, "Taste and see that the Lord is good," felt odd to share under the circumstances. So I stood there wrestling with God, listing all the reasons this wasn't a good idea, while worship drew to a close. I realised that I had a choice: either obey God, or miss this moment. Almost unconsciously, my feet started moving.

By the time I reached Mariah, worship was nearly over. I didn't want to announce the verse publicly, so I leaned down and quietly whispered it in her ear. Both Alicia and my pastor's wife looked at me, so I felt led to share the verse with Alicia as well.

Alicia's eyes widened. "Do you want to know what I just prayed?" she asked. When I answered yes, Alicia explained, "I asked God to stop the enemy from whispering in Mariah's ear and allow only His voice to be heard. When I opened my eyes, I saw you standing in front of her, and you leaned over, whispering a Bible verse in her ear." We both stood there in awe, recognising how perfectly God had orchestrated everything to the second.

God's timing was flawless. I didn't move until the very last song, and yet He ensured I would be in front of Mariah at the exact moment Alicia opened her eyes. That's something only God can do. He touched all three of us that morning, gently guiding me and filling me with the courage to obey. He strengthened Alicia's faith in her prayers, and most importantly,

He gave Mariah a personal and timely invitation to experience Him for herself.

Since my deliverance, I truly hear God's leading in ways I never did before. I'm learning to step into uncomfortable situations, trusting His purpose and timing. With His strength, I can listen and respond, even when I don't understand. Thank you, Jesus, for setting me free.

**Jeremiah 1:7-9**

But the lord said to me: "Do not say, "I am a youth; For you shall go to all to whom I send you, And whatever I command you, you shall speak. Do not be afraid of their faces, For I am with you to deliver you, says the Lord. Then the lord put forth His hand and touched my mouth, and the Lord said to me: "Behold, I have put my words in your mouth.

# Chosen Like His Mama

My youngest son, Colton, was eleven when I wrote this book, but his journey with God started even earlier. At just seven years old, Colton began to hear God's voice. He was saved outside of the church, just as I was, and God called both of our names at the same time. Colton is no exception when it comes to being chosen—God is already shaping him, drawing him close, and speaking to him in ways I recognise from my own childhood.

The very week my dreams of my mother began, Colton started asking, "Why don't we go to church? Can we go to church?" I was stunned. Where were these questions coming from? Only later would I realise that God was reaching out to both of us at the same time—a perfect confirmation of His timing.

Sometimes, when I sense an evil presence near Colton, he will come running to me within a minute or two, already aware that something spiritual is happening. He not only senses when something is wrong but often knows exactly what it is. At only eleven, he understands the difference between battles of the flesh and spiritual warfare. In those moments, Colton will come to me and ask for prayer. When I ask him what for, he'll say, "That stupid demon thinks he can talk to me." Sometimes he'll even share troubling thoughts about harm coming to his family or himself. This breaks my heart, but I've learned to ask God, "Why do You allow these demons to speak to my children? I'm doing everything I know to protect them."

But the Lord gently replied, "Don't you understand? This is a victory. The devil and his demons are going to speak—even Jesus was tempted by the devil. You and your children are not exempt from spiritual attacks." God showed me that Colton is being prepared for spiritual battles, learning to discern the enemy's voice from his own. He knows when a thought isn't his, who is speaking, and what he needs to do about it. This is why it's so important to teach our children from a young age how to fight in the Spirit.

One evening, I was in the kitchen making dinner when I sensed the Lord telling me, "Take a picture of everyone in the living room." I didn't understand why, but I obeyed. The picture seemed completely normal—until I noticed that Colton was upset. When I asked him what was wrong, he began to cry, asking why God would let something so awful happen. He said that he thought men were coming to our house to shoot us, and that God knew and was letting it happen. He told me, "God doesn't care about us." This was all happening in the early days of our salvation, before Colton understood the reality of spiritual warfare, and before the devil's tactics were as apparent to us.

Puzzled, I picked up my phone and zoomed in on Colton in the photo. That's when I saw it: in the picture, a python was wrapped around his head with its mouth against his ear. In this instance, the demonic presence was outside of him rather than inside, but I realised it doesn't really matter—the outcome should always be the same. The enemy must go.

Distracted by dinner, I had almost missed it. I quickly oiled my hand, walked over to Colton, and placed my hand on his head, commanding the serpent's head to be cut off in Jesus' name. I reassured Colton: "This wasn't you—it was the enemy trying to plant doubt in your mind about God's love." I showed Colton the picture because he needed to understand that this battle is real. Don't shy away from telling your children the truth. If you don't, the devil will exploit their ignorance. God says, "My people perish for lack of knowledge."

One night, on the drive home from church, I was discussing with my husband how God already knows who will be saved and who won't. My husband struggled with this idea, arguing that it must interfere with free will, and we both got frustrated. Colton was nowhere near this conversation—he wasn't listening and couldn't have known what we were debating.

About an hour later, Colton came to me and said, "God told me to ask you what John 18:36 means." We looked up the verse together and, remarkably, it offered the exact explanation I had been trying to give my husband. When I shared this with my friend Nikki, she immediately knew what had happened. She gently said, "It could be that God couldn't speak directly to you while you were frustrated, so He used your child." Her words corrected and encouraged me, reminding me how important it is to keep our hearts open.

As women, sometimes it's hard to submit our hearts or lay down our pride. In that moment, I wanted to give up, but God still had a way to speak to me—through my own child. I repented and pray that I'll never close myself off to God's voice again.

I am so excited to see what God has planned for Colton's life. I know it's going to be nothing short of amazing to watch.

**Psalm 78:4**

We will not hide them from their children, Telling to the generation to come the praises of the Lord, And his strength and His wonderful works that He has done.

**John 18:36**

Jesus answered, "My kingdom is not of this world. If my kingdom were of this world, My servants would fight, so that I should not be delivered to the Jews, but now my kingdom is not from here."

# Praying purpose into her Life

My daughter, Brittany, was fifteen when she began attending church with me, the second of my children to experience salvation. At first, she would sit with her cousin in the back row, hardly engaged, showing little interest in being there, and never participating in worship. During this period, I received a call from Brittany's school requesting a meeting. My heart sank as I learned that Brittany had been secretly self-harming, cutting her wrists and hiding the scars beneath her bracelets. The news was devastating; fear and guilt overwhelmed me. How had I, her mother, missed the signs of her suffering?

A teacher had noticed Brittany's pain, and soon she began counselling and was prescribed medication. The process was terrifying for both of us. Later, Brittany confided that her actions weren't because of depression, but from a relentless urge to see blood—a compulsion so powerful it wouldn't abate until she saw it. I recognised immediately that this was a spiritual battle.

Around this challenging time, our church announced an upcoming youth camp. I desperately wanted Brittany to go, knowing it could be life-changing for her, but convincing her wouldn't be easy. The cost was $250—a significant sum when our family's finances were tight, and my husband's condition was deteriorating. Even if I managed to secure the money, Brittany had no desire to attend. Regardless, I knew deep down she needed to be there.

As camp approached, Brittany's youth pastor texted me. He said the church wanted Brittany to be part of the camp so much that they would cover her full expenses. I was amazed and grateful—we had only attended this church for less than a year and still barely knew anyone. To help Brittany feel more comfortable, I persuaded her cousin Robin to attend as well, which finally convinced Brittany to go.

I prayed for her every day she was at camp. The week stretched from Monday to Friday, and by Thursday morning, I felt a sudden, urgent need to pray for her. Parents were asked not to contact their children at camp so they wouldn't get homesick, so

I had no idea how she was really doing: whether she stayed in the back or ventured forward. As I began to pray, my words shifted. I found myself speaking things I hadn't planned— words that sounded like prophecy, though I didn't realise it at the time. I prayed over Brittany's life with a conviction that surprised me, declaring she would lead her generation.

To this day, others have come to Brittany, telling her she is destined to be a leader—echoing those very words spoken in prayer. On Friday morning, Brittany's pastor's wife texted me: "I just wanted to let you know that Brittany is doing amazing and has asked to be baptised tomorrow." My heart overflowed with gratitude for these wonderful people God placed in our lives.

When Brittany returned home, she was transformed. For the first time, she was smiling, willingly talking with me, and confessing that while she initially disliked camp, by the end she felt drawn to worship. She described an evening at the altar when, desperate to be free, she looked up to see a woman from the church praying for her. That woman later told me she had gone in search of Brittany at the altar, amid the crowded room. Suddenly, the crowd parted, and she saw Brittany standing directly in front of her. The woman described seeing, in the spirit, a long arm reach from Brittany's chest, beckoning her to come. She said she had never witnessed anything like it before.

On the last day, as the kids were baptised in the lake, Brittany went through the line. Emerging from the water, she felt a strange, physical sensation in her heart, as if it were being healed and restored. Compelled to go again, she entered the water a second time—this time her legs gave way, and they had to help her out. In that moment, she knew God had set her free; her chains were broken, and the darkness that had haunted her was gone. Brittany came home truly changed—filled with peace and joy. She now worships passionately, reads her Bible, prays, and lives with a renewed sense of purpose. She no longer needs medication.

Today, Brittany notices when other teens are struggling with self-harm. Sometimes, God will point someone out to her as we're out and about, and she will reach out to them. I believe Brittany was created for such a time as this and will lead many others to freedom. Thank you, Jesus.

## 1 Corinthians 14:3

But he who prophesies speaks edification and exhortation and comfort to men.

## Esther 4:14

For if you remain completely silent at this time, relief and deliverance will arise for the Jews from another place, but you and your father's house will perish. Yet who knows whether you have come to the kingdom for such a time as this?

## Deuteronomy 26:8

So the Lord brought us out of Egypt with a mighty hand and with an outstretched arm, with great terror and with signs, and wonders.

# My son's second chance

A couple of months after my daughter received salvation, my oldest son, Dylan, experienced his own decisive breakthrough—he was both saved and delivered on the same day. It was a Sunday morning. I was getting ready to leave for church when Dylan walked in after a night out, still feeling the effects of drinking. Despite his condition, he looked at me and said, "Wait, I'm going with you."

My first instinct was hesitation—I thought, There's no way I'm taking you to church like this. As I was about to tell him to wait and come later that evening, I felt the Lord nudge me: "Take him." I wrestled internally, thinking, What will everyone think? But again, God's voice was clear: "Take him." So I did.

On the way to church, Dylan unexpectedly opened up about the heavy battle he was facing that morning. He confessed he was struggling with intense suicidal thoughts, and that a voice was urging him to drive into oncoming traffic. He admitted he was scared he might act on those impulses. Though Dylan had come to church with me before, I could always tell he was reluctant to be there.

We arrived at church, and although I noticed people glancing in our direction, it no longer mattered to me. During worship, Dylan made his way to the altar and began to pray. Before long, others gathered around him, laying hands and speaking freedom over his life. I was on the other side of the altar so that I couldn't see everything, but I could sense that something powerful was happening.

After worship, back at our seats, Dylan looked transformed— relieved and at peace. After the service, a lady approached Dylan and explained that she'd witnessed everything and saw a demon leave him. She told him his face changed physically, and after that, she saw three crosses appear on his face. That day marked the end of his struggle with suicidal thoughts.

For about a year, Dylan was on fire for the Lord, faithfully attending church and pursuing God passionately. But just as suddenly, he slipped back into old patterns and distanced himself from the church. It was a sobering reminder of how quickly things can shift in the spiritual realm. For about a year,

Dylan didn't want to hear anything about God and got defensive if anyone brought it up.

Then, unexpectedly, Dylan started asking about God again. Over a few months, he became increasingly curious—asking questions, initiating conversations about faith, and eventually, returning to church. Now, he experiences God in new ways. He's shared with me that, on many mornings during his commute, he feels as if God is downloading entire sermons into his mind.

Like me, Dylan also sees in the spirit. I'm encouraged and excited to see where God will lead my son next.

**Acts 16:31**

So they said,"Believe on the Lord Jesus Christ, and you will be saved, you and your household."

## Psalm 34:17

The righteous cry out, and the Lord hears, And delivers them out of all their troubles.

## Jeremiah 29:11

For I know the thoughts that I think toward you, says the Lord, thoughts of peace and not of evil, to give you a future and a hope.

# God's promise over my son.

My fourteen-year-old son, Ryan, is a precious gift. He's always belonged to God, and though he's under the age of accountability because of his severe nonverbal autism, I've never once felt angry at God for his condition. Even before I genuinely believed, gratitude for Ryan filled my heart. I often asked myself—what if Ryan had been placed with a family less able to love and care for him? He is safe with us, and that's more than enough. Yes, life can be challenging; caring for Ryan means planning every detail, even for small outings. But our love for him always outweighs the difficulties.

Not long after I was saved, as I was lying in bed, I sensed an evil presence. It offered a tempting promise: "If you stop what you're doing right now, I will fully heal Ryan." Without hesitation, I rebuked it. That moment showed me two things. First, the devil only imitates—he tries to steal what God offers. Second, if the enemy is promising healing, that's a clue that God's healing for Ryan is certain. The enemy lies, but if you listen closely, you often discover God's truth in the opposite. I now know with complete confidence that God has promised Ryan's healing—one day, my son will speak the gospel with his own voice.

When I pray for Ryan, I hear, "He is healed because of your faith." This always brings back a memory of my father. When I was a child, my dad suffered a stroke and couldn't move his ankle. For over a year, our family and church prayed for his healing. I remember feeling frustrated, watching my dad go up for prayer week after week. One day, I asked, "Why do you keep asking?  Gods not going to heal you?" My dad gently replied, "God already healed me—it's my faith that needs to catch up." Eventually, he was healed during a service, and I witnessed that miracle firsthand. God used that journey to show me that persistence in faith matters; keep knocking, and He will answer. Now, God is telling me to receive Ryan's healing with the same perseverance and faith.

Since our salvation, many have prayed for Ryan. I've watched seasoned pastors stop mid-prayer and declare, "This is a lie from the pit of hell"—without even knowing Ryan's story. They all agree: autism does not define my son. I have come out of agreement with his diagnosis. We've prayed, rebuked, and claimed victory, especially after I read the story in the Bible about the mute boy who would throw himself into the fire. I realised then that some things labelled as autism were really spiritual in nature.

Ryan used to try to touch hot stovetops, burning himself repeatedly—no matter how we wanted to protect him. After we prayed for deliverance, that compulsion disappeared completely. For years, it was a daily struggle, but now, the dangerous behaviour is gone. We can attend church together; Ryan listens to worship music, makes eye contact, and his joy is undeniable. In my heart, I know the Holy Spirit dwells in him.

We've even brought Ryan to revivals, including the Northern Georgia revival where Isaiah Saldivar was preaching one night. We even got into the immersion pools he was in. Ryan even took his pillow in the water. God gave our family peace during those special times. It hasn't always been easy, but through every challenge, God shows His goodness. I believe all chains have been broken, and Ryan is entirely free.

So now I ask: would you agree with me in faith? I trust that my faith will continue to grow until I see Ryan's complete healing manifested. I can't wait to introduce Ryan to the world and say,

"Look what the Lord has done!" One day, you'll hear him speak—and share the good news for himself.

### John 9:1-3

1Now as Jesus passed by, He saw a man who was blind from birth. 2 And His disciples asked Him, saying, "Rabbi, who sinned, this man or his parent, that he was born blind? 3 Jesus answered, " Neither this man nor his parents sinned, but that the works of God should be revealed in him.

# When my song reached heaven

My husband's testimony is truly remarkable. Even as I write this, I feel the Lord stirring my heart about my next book—the story of my husband's journey from the pit of hell into God's presence. To say his journey was eventful would be an understatement. When you look at Brent, you see Jesus unmistakably; nothing else can explain the transformation in him.

Brent battled a generational stronghold of alcoholism. The demon attached to his lineage had been with his family for generations and had no intention of letting go. I know this intimately, not only because I lived with Brent, but because I also contended with this demon myself. We were not on friendly terms. I hated that demon in a way that's hard to articulate. I recognised precisely what I was up against. Before I was saved, Brent's drinking didn't trouble me, but everything changed after my salvation—especially when I was filled with the Holy Spirit. I often wondered exactly what shifted as the demon began manifesting more around me.

Was it reacting to the Holy Spirit, or was the Holy Spirit giving me discernment? That year was long and complicated, and the demon grew more aggressive each day. I'd anoint the kitchen table before Brent came home, so most dinners would be accompanied by his low growls—not the dramatic kind you see in movies, but a quiet growl whenever I spoke. I'd also anoint Brent's bed, his pillow, and even him while he slept. Once he'd fallen asleep, he'd start growling much louder. It wore on my nerves, so I would get my Bible and read aloud to him. Looking back, it's a bit humorous—I figured if the demon could bother me, I'd return the favour.

This spirit hated me more than I expected. On some level, I knew it was there and also realised I couldn't drive it out while Brent was still in agreement with it, so I did what I could to ease my own mind. One day, I took a cloth anointed by Brittany's youth pastor and women from our church, cut it into pieces, and taped them inside Brent's work boots. That night, after Brent was asleep, I heard a voice come out of him that was not his own: "I'm going to kill you." I rebuked it in Jesus' name, shaken but determined. I texted my friend for advice. She replied, "They always say that. You're covered in the blood; it can't harm you."

The next day, I anointed more cloths and taped them into all his shoes. After that, the demon never spoke to me again. I'm so grateful for God's protection—I know that thing could have killed me.

There was one particular night at dinner when Brent excused himself to use the restroom. While he was gone, I pleaded the blood of Jesus over his food. Demons do not like that. Brent returned, took a bite, made a face of pure disgust, forced down another bite, then got up and walked to the trash can. When I asked what was wrong, he just said, "I don't know—I feel terrible." I told him, "While you were gone, I pleaded the blood of Jesus over your food." The look of fear on his face said it all. He rushed to the bathroom and violently threw up.

I was panicking, so I reached out to my pastor's wife. She probably thought I was losing it, but she gently reassured me that Jesus' blood covered me. I confided everything to her, and as wild as it all seemed, every word was accurate. I've seen

Brent's eyes shift into snake eyes; I've watched his face contort under spiritual oppression.

During that time, I developed a unique worship style. There's one specific song I love, and whenever I sing it in worship, my husband is always on my heart. I did this nearly every day. There's something supernatural about my worship—it's how I connect most deeply with God. For over a year, this one song became my anchor. Every time I worshipped, I thought about Brent, interceding for him, pouring out my heart to God through song. It was only this song that carried such passion and connection for me.

Eventually, some men from the church and my oldest son, Dylan, encouraged Brent to go to a men's encounter—a three-day retreat. I was shocked when he agreed. My excitement was off the charts. The morning he left, he was already suffering significant withdrawal symptoms, and I had no idea what to expect. I prayed nonstop for him.

When Brent came back home, he was a new man. He looked amazing. He told me that during worship, the very first song brought him to the altar—every withdrawal melted away. Something profound happened during that song, though he couldn't recall its name. The next day, he found the song at work and came home to share the name with me. Remarkably, I was playing it in our house at that exact moment.

He said, "This is the song!" I could hardly believe it. I replied, "This is my song—I've been singing it to the Lord every day for over a year!" I never played it when Brent was around; I always did it during his work hours. God had heard my cry. That song became a vessel God used to reach my husband. Only the Lord could orchestrate something so intimate and meaningful. It's a reminder that what's done in secret will be revealed, that God treasures our private worship and can use it in miraculous ways.

For me, it's a song between the three of us—God, my husband, and me. It's beautiful. God is faithful and truly good, all the time

### 1 Kings 3:9

Therefore give to Your servant an understanding heart to judge Your people, that I may discern between good and evil. For who is ablem to judge this great people of Yours?

## Psalms 126:5-6

**5** Those who sow tears shall reap in joy. 6 He who continually goes forth weeping, Bearing seed for sowing, shall doubtless comes again with rejoicing, Bringing his sheaves with him

## Matthew 6:6

But you, when you pray, go into your room, and when you have shut your door, pray to your Father who is in the secret place; and your Father who sees in secret will reward you openly.

## Acts 16:31

So they said," Believe on the Lord Jesus Christ, and you will be saved, you and your household."

# Freedom in the Midnight Hour

My husband's newfound freedom was painfully short-lived. Within just a couple of weeks, he was drinking again. That period was the most challenging for me. I cannot fully express what I was feeling. For three precious weeks, I had the husband God had created just for me—and in an instant, he was gone. During those weeks, he was everything I'd ever wanted. So when the old Brent returned, it felt like a slap in the face.

I remember the exact moment he came back. Brent walked into the house after work, and the expression on his face said it all: "I'm back." It was as if the demon was proud of itself. I hated the way I felt around him—like my very skin was crawling. Through all that pain, though, I wasn't angry with my husband. I knew who the enemy was.

A couple more weeks passed. One night, Brent came home from work and literally fell out of his truck. I realised this demon was going to kill him. I was so upset that I got into my car and just drove. I ended up not far away, parked in a church parking lot. I sat there sobbing and screaming. I told God, "I don't want to do this anymore. I can't!" I cried out, telling God

I was done fighting—I couldn't battle this demon any longer. I said, "God, if you don't go into the pit of hell and bring him out, he will die. Are you going to save him or not?"

Suddenly, peace overtook me. The crying and shaking stopped, and I was completely calm. Now, I understand that in that moment, I truly gave the battle to the Lord. Until then, I'd wanted the victory for saving my husband myself, but I finally understood this was God's battle. I put my trust in Him, stepped back, and God stepped forward.

I drove home and went inside. Brent looked at me with a smirk I can't stand, and said something like, "You all better now?" Right then, I knew it wasn't my husband speaking, but something else. It was as if God adjusted my emotions so they couldn't be shaken. Smiling, I replied, "I'm great. How are you?" The confusion on Brent's face was priceless. The demon inside him understood that it was no longer fighting against me, but against God Himself. Brent avoided me for the rest of the night.

About a month later, another men's encounter event took place. Brent went and came back completely free again. That very night, we went to bed as usual, but I woke up in the middle of the night to Brent screaming. He was fighting something I couldn't see, crying out for help. Through panic, he told me there was a black figure on top of him, choking him. Instinctively, I began praying, commanding every demon to leave in Jesus' name—as I'd learned through my dreams. Brent calmed down, but immediately started having a panic attack and desperately wanted his Bible. He refused to take mine and liked his, so we went outside to retrieve it together. He grabbed his Bible, opened it, put it on his chest—and within seconds, he said, "Okay, it's gone." That was the last time we ever saw that demon. Brent is a different person now.

Brent's struggle was never really with his flesh; he was fighting a demon that gained access through alcohol. If you're caught doing something you don't want to do, it may not be you—it's something spiritual. Brent will tell you that he never has to resist the idea of drinking anymore; it simply doesn't cross his mind. We've spoken with many people in recovery from alcohol who stopped through programs, and they consistently say that the thoughts and cravings persist daily. These people have learned to control the demon's influence, but the demon still longs for a drink, so unless it is commanded to go, the thoughts remain. When you take authority and command the demon to leave, the torment will stop.

As of writing this, Brent has been sober for nearly a year and a half. He owns his own flooring business and freely shares his testimony with customers, always pointing them to God. Most evenings, he comes home telling me about conversations he's had—always about God. He now serves at the same men's encounter event where he found freedom, and recently returned from a mission trip to Mexico. God has truly set him apart, and I believe He will use Brent extensively throughout his life.

In our journey to freedom, perhaps the best advice I ever received was from my pastor: "Stop declaring your husband is an alcoholic. Start declaring he is a child of God." I took that advice to heart. Every day, I declared out loud that Brent is a child of God, chosen before the foundation of the earth was laid, and set apart for a purpose. Declare this blessing over your lost loved ones—stop speaking death, and talk about life.

## 2 Timothy 4:18

And the Lord will deliver me from every evil work and preserve me for His heavenly kingdom. To Him be glory forever and ever Amen.

## Exodus 14:14

The Lord will fight for you, and you shall hold your peace.

## Matthew 12:43-45

43 "When an unclean spirit goes out of a man, he goes through dry places, seeking rest, and finds none. 44 Then he says," I will return to my house from which I came: And when he comes, he finds it empty, swept, and put in order. 45 Then he goes and takes with him seven other spirits more wicked than himself, and they enter and dwell there. And the last state of the man is worse than the first. So shall it also be with this wicked generation."

# The demon that can't hide

My husband is free and will never go back. That doesn't mean that the stupid demon never shows up. From time to time, it checks in, almost as if it's seeing whether the house is empty again.

What this demon doesn't understand is that God has marked it for me. Since I've been saved, God has given me a beautiful gift to protect my family and others. I don't fully know what to call it. It's similar to discernment, but it feels like more than that. I haven't yet met anyone else quite like me in this area, and I'm hoping this book helps me build relationships with others who operate in similar gifts.

I know when demons are around. Sometimes I know exactly what kind of demon it is; other times, I just know that something evil has entered the room. I can even tell the difference between a demon and a witch. A demon feels like pure, concentrated evil, while a witch still feels evil, but there's a sense of humanity there—it feels like a person. It's hard to explain.

God has marked the demon that tried to destroy my family and kill my husband—almost like He put a fingerprint on it. It carries an undeniable feeling that I recognize instantly. God knows it will try to come back, and He's given me a weapon of discernment against it.

Since that demon was cast out, my husband has only had one thought about drinking. He was driving home when it happened. He said it was literally a split second before he took the thought captive. When he walked in the door that day, I could feel that demon. I knew it would only be there for one reason.

So I asked him, "Have you been thinking about drinking?"

At first, he said no. I looked at him and replied, "Don't lie to me." The look on his face said everything. Then he admitted yes, told me what had happened, and said it was only a few seconds before he shut the thought down.

He asked me, "How did you know?"

I told him, "I'm not sure—I just do."

We prayed together, commanded it to leave, and declared that it is not allowed to be around us or our home. I believe God marked that demon because it's a generational spirit. It thinks it has a right to us—to my husband, to me, to my children.

These demons don't give up easily. But God has a plan for my family, and He has given us weapons to fight with. His plans will come to pass—the devil loses in this story. God is so good.

### Genesis 4:7

If you do well, will you not accepted? And if you do not do well, sin lies at the door. And its desire is for you, but you should rule over it.

### 1 Corinthians 12:10

To another the working of miracles, to another prophecy, to another discerning of spirits, to another different kinds of tongues, to another the interpretation of tongues.

### 2 Thessalonians 3:3

But the Lord is faithful, who will establish you and guard you from the evil one.

# Cancelling the assignment

I was driving to church one morning with my kids. Brent drove separately that day. On the way, I had a thought: If the kids and I were killed in a wreck, would Brent backslide?

I never have these thoughts. I wondered for a few seconds. Then I had another thought: You'd better not come into agreement with that. I rebuked the idea in Jesus' name.

Neither thought was mine. The devil was trying to get me to enter into a contract with him. When he gives you an idea, the deal doesn't activate because you said yes; it is active because you didn't take the thought captive, and you let it start building.

God was right there with me to lead me. The light revealed the darkness that was trying to operate.

I made it to church just fine. I was in Ryan's class that day, so I didn't get to go to service. What I didn't know was that after church, the pastor had an altar call for husbands and dads to come up and pray for protection over their families.

I left the church, and my husband was in the truck in front of me. He pulled out; I pulled down to be the next one out. My car was stopped, waiting on the traffic. A truck came off the road and hit my vehicle.

At the exact moment the car hit me, Ryan got out of his seat and leaned between the two front seats. If he hadn't, he would have been hurt—it hit his door hard.

When it first happened, I couldn't think at all. I was just shocked. I don't know what I was or who I was. I was out of it. With that being said, I had another thought that I didn't see how possible it was, because my brain wasn't functioning.

I didn't wonder whether I would make heaven. I had regret. I remember telling God I was sorry—that I could have done so much more for Him. What a waste. In that moment, I didn't know we were all fine; for all I knew, this was it.

I didn't want to leave—not because I don't want to be in heaven, but because I want to do everything He has for me. When I leave this world and stand before Him, I want to know I did everything He said I would do. Nothing missing; I am what He says I am.

My car was totaled, and we walked away with only a few minor marks.

What would have happened if I hadn't rebuked the thought? If I hadn't taken that thought captive, then I would have agreed to being killed that day. What if I had refused to hear God that morning when He stepped in?

Thoughts are not just harmless imaginations; they are where everything starts. Take complete control over every thought that enters your mind. Do not allow yourself to daydream. Take every thought captive, examine it, and judge where it came from

**2 Corinthians 10:5**

Casting down arguments and every high thing that exalts itself against the knowledge of God, bringing every thought into captivity to the obedience of Christ,

# Can't you remember

I was invited to a church service in Potosi, MO, by my good friend Stacy. I have a bad habit of being quick to judge. It's just how I was raised—to test every spirit, which isn't a bad thing. The Bible tells us to test every spirit. At the same time, you'd better be careful when you say, "This isn't the Holy Spirit." His ways are not our ways. That's why discernment is necessary. You can't learn discernment; it's a gift.

Worship starts, and people begin acting in ways I don't like. Then this man runs up in front of me. He's running, bent over and to the side.

I'll be honest—it was creepy. I'd never been to this church before. So I start praying, "God, is this You? Do I leave or stay?"

I get a thought that's not mine. It came with the sweetest feeling. It made me want to fall into His arms and weep. It said, "Can't you remember?"

My eyes filled with tears, and I said, "Yes, God, I remember." My parents would take me to churches like this when I was little. I remembered my mom and my Aunt Sue running the aisles, hands flying in the air, crying out in tongues. "Yes, God, I remember."

I'm so glad I stayed, because the preaching was better than the worship, which is hard to find nowadays. The message was strong; it was on the Word of God.

He preached about how to better distinguish between the wheat and the tares. How you can only tell the difference if you're serving the true Jesus? How God allow both to prosper for His will? How can you know? Because one will stand behind the cross, the whole service is focused on God's Word. The other is stuck on themselves.

Phones will be out, taking pictures of them laying hands on people. They'll spend an hour on worship, ten minutes preaching, then an altar call for the supernatural. They desire the paranormal more than God's truth. They want to make things happen.

What's happening is that people go to a church service to see a particular person, hoping that person will lay hands on them, thinking that person has the power to heal. If you're not going to church for God and God alone, you're in error.

You can go to service after service, have all the supernatural things happen, and remain unchanged. Only the Word of God, being eaten and digested, will change you.

This man preached and preached truth; it was the most holy preaching I've ever heard. After he was done, there was no altar call. He said he knew the Word of God went out and was planted that night, and he didn't need to put his hands all over it.

I believe in intercessory prayer and the laying on of hands, but somewhere along the line, we forget that God's Word is enough.

To God be the glory. I'm so glad God told me to stay and changed the way I was looking at some things.

**John 7:18**

He who speaks from himself seeks his own glory; but He who seeks the glory of the One who sent Him is true, and no unrighteousness is in Him

**Hebrews 5:14**

But solid food belongs to those who are of full age, that is, those who by reason of use have their senses exercised to discern both good and evil

# Vision

I've had one open vision—that's what I believe it's called. It happened on a Friday night at a meeting in the Good News Coffee Shop in Bonne Terre.

We had a powerful service, as we usually do on Friday nights. After it ended, people began to leave until only about six of us remained. We began worshipping again, and in that moment, God stepped into the room with us. Everyone was having their own personal experience with the Lord.

My experience was beautiful and deepened my understanding. I don't believe God shows us things for entertainment; there is always wisdom and purpose in a vision.

In the vision, I saw my own body lying on the ground. I knew the body was dead. I looked at it with absolutely no attachment, as if it were just a dirty outfit I had taken off. Then I saw a hand, almost as large as my body, reach down inside that body and pull another "me" out.

I didn't see anything else with my natural eyes, but I understood that I was now standing next to the Lord. I knew He was separating me for what He had called me to do—showing me that if I truly wanted to pick up my cross and follow Him, it would cost me everything I understood about this world. He was revealing that the things of this world are nothing compared to what He has for me.

While all of this was happening, everyone else in the room was also in their own moment with the Lord. Then, at the same time, we all stopped. Pastor Allen simply said, "We just entered the heavenly realm." And I knew he was right. Yes, we did.

If you haven't yet had a chance to come to the Good News Coffee Shop in Bonne Terre, we meet most Friday nights at 6:30. You should definitely go and see what God has for you.

**James 2:26**

"For as the body without the spirit is dead, so faith without works is dead also."

# Ryan's prayer  Dreams

I prayed for Ryan one night at church because he was getting upset. I knew that if he didn't calm down, I would have to leave with him, so I whispered a quick, simple prayer in my mind: I asked God to give him peace. Within just a few seconds, Ryan was calm, with a big smile on his face.

That night, I found myself wondering what really happens when God gives someone peace. What is going on in the spirit realm that we can't see? That same night, God answered my question with a very vivid dream.

In the dream, I was lying in a hospital bed. I had just come to, and I was agitated because I didn't know what had happened to me. I started to cry and demanded that someone tell me what was wrong. Suddenly, a tall man was sitting at the end of my bed. He had a guitar in his hands and began to play the most beautiful song I had ever heard.

The song was alive. Every word wrapped around me like the most comforting hug. As he sang, all my fear and anxiety melted away, replaced by pure joy. I asked him, "Are you an angel?" He replied, "Yes. God sent me to bring you peace."

I woke up and immediately wrote down the dream. I was not about to take any chances on forgetting this one. God says, "If you lack wisdom, ask, and it will be given." I had wondered, What happens when someone prays for peace? And He gave me wisdom to understand. He really is a great Teacher.

Now Ryan is getting to the point where I have to be careful what I pray over him, because when I pray for peace, he often gets so excited at church that he starts laughing really loudly. So I've stopped praying specifically for "peace" for him in that way and instead pray for a calmness to rest on him.

God hasn't given me the dream that explains that prayer yet. I can't wait to have it.

### Psalm 29:11

" The LORD will give strength to His people; the LORD will bless His people with peace."

# Colton's prayer dream

I went to Springfield, MO, one night for a service called Arise Nights. A couple of friends had invited me. During the service, I went up for prayer.

When the man started praying for me, my arms began to shake. Then I let out a strange scream, jumped like a frog, and fell to the floor. I honestly don't know how else to describe it—that's precisely what happened. That's all I've got.

That night, I had a vivid dream. In the dream, a man about eight feet tall was walking toward me. He was holding a spear lifted high into the air—it was as tall as he was. At the end of the spear was a dead python. The man never said a word. He simply walked up and laid the dead python at my feet.

Over the next couple of days, I noticed something unusual. Colton, my child who had always struggled with behaviour issues, was suddenly being kind. I started trying to remember the last time I'd had to correct him, and I realised—it was the day I went to Springfield. This was a child who had to be corrected daily. Now he was being really nice, even sweet. There was a significant change in his behaviour.

I began to understand that the deliverance that happened to me in that church service might not have been for me personally— it was for my child. I still don't know precisely how all of this works. All I know is that God may have used my body for the deliverance, but the freedom belonged to my son.

We stand in the gap and pray for the sick all the time—so why couldn't we also stand in for the deliverance of our children, or even anyone else God places on our hearts? We will never fully understand God's ways; we simply can't.

What did I learn from this? Never put God in a box. Never assume He can't move in a certain way. Who are we to say what God can or cannot do? He can do whatever He wants, whenever He wants, and however He wants.

My response is: more of God—even when I don't understand it.

## Psalm 143:12

In Your mercy cut off my enemies, And destroy all those who afflict my soul; For I am Your servant.

# Brents dream

When Brent backslid after that first men's encounter, it was devastating. I remember praying and asking God, "Why would You show me what I could have, then let it be taken away?" It hurt deeply. God didn't answer me with words. Instead, He gave me an eye-opening dream that revealed how desperately demons desire to be with us.

After the dream, I understood something in a new way: God truly sets us free, but we still have choices. When we go back to our old sin—to our own "vomit"—we are the ones opening the door and giving the demonic a warm welcome back home.

In the dream, it was nighttime. I was standing on a roof, looking across the street into my own house. Inside, I saw my family sitting together in the living room, laughing and enjoying one another. I knew, somehow, that I had just been cast out of myself. I was completely confused, because up until that moment, I thought I *was* me—but now I realised I wasn't actually Angie at all.

What struck me most was that I didn't care who I truly was. All I cared about was getting back to that family. In the dream, they were mine. I would do anything to be with them again.

I began pleading with God: "If You let me go back, I'll be good. They won't even know I'm there. I won't say a word, I won't hurt them—I'll just watch them. I promise." The separation from them was unbearable. It felt physically painful, worse than the grief of losing a loved one in death. The ache of being cut off from them was torment.

God answered, "I can't let you go back. Even if you kept your word, just your presence in their life would destroy them. You would alter what I have for them. You would take them off course."

In the dream, I still didn't care. The grief and longing were so intense that I started looking for another way back. I thought, *They want me there. They need me. I have to get back to them.*

One of the most powerful parts of this dream was seeing how God interacted with that demon. He wasn't screaming or raging. He was talking. He was trying to help it understand. He had compassion, even for it. He knew it hurt, and He was trying to give it comfort.

That's the way He tells *us* to treat our enemies.

In that dream, I saw that God truly is a loving God—even toward those who are evil. It also showed me something else: these demons have nothing to do except try to find a way back in. That is their constant goal.

You'd better not give the devil a place. Because yes—even a Christian can open a door and provide a place for him.

After this dream, I understood more clearly why returning to old sin is so dangerous. We aren't just slipping up—we are inviting back what God, in His mercy, once drove out.

**Matthew 12:43-45**

43"When an unclean spirit goes out of a man, he goes through dry places, seeking rest, and finds none.44Then he says, 'I will return to my house from which I came.' And when he comes, he finds it empty, swept, and put in order. 45Then he goes and takes with him seven other spirits more wicked than himself, and they enter and dwell there; and the last state of that man is worse than the first. So shall it also be with this wicked generation."

# Rapture dream

I had a vivid dream of the rapture—or maybe it was simply my appointed time in the dream. I was walking through a town, an empty village where everything was black and white. It felt like the beginning of a bad dream.

I looked up and cried out to God in anger. I said, "I don't want to be with them; I want You. Only You." I remember how desperately I wanted to be with God—more than anything I've ever experienced. It's hard to explain, but in the dream, it was like I knew Him on another level that doesn't make sense in this world. In that moment, I was saying, "I need a time-out. Even if it's just for a second, I need to be with You."

Then the most incredible thing happened. It felt like I was shot out of my body like a bullet fired from a gun. I was going so fast—like the speed of light. I remember the force of it and how it was a perfectly straight line upward.

I also remember understanding that He wasn't going to let me see anything on the way—or maybe I just wasn't allowed to remember what I saw. I went so far up that I felt a million miles away from my body, yet somehow I could still feel both places at once.

All of a sudden, I began to fall back toward my body. The way down was fast, but not as fast as the way up. Going up was a straight shot; coming back down, I was tumbling over and over. I was aware of a cord attached to me and wondered how I wasn't getting tangled in it.

I couldn't see anything solid at first, but I knew an angel was taking me back. I was fully aware of his presence. I started begging God, "At least let me see the angel. I know he's there."

Then I could see him. He had massive wings and was directly in front of me, holding me with his arm as he carried me downward. I didn't see his face. When the Lord let me see him clearly, it was like being at the eye doctor, looking into the machine—at first, you see nothing, and then, slowly, it all comes into focus.

I believe I was seeing the veil, and God thinned it just enough for me to glimpse what was usually hidden. There are so many angels around us, and we never know it because of that veil.

On the way down, while the veil was thin, I also saw a small opening at the top of the sky with bright light pouring through it. I saw the spirits of people being pulled up through that opening. It reminded me of how a vacuum sucks things up.

When I came back to my body, the landing was hard. In the dream, it felt like I slammed off a building and hit the ground. The second I landed, I was wide awake—lying in bed, trying to understand what had just happened. I couldn't get over how completely awake I was after being in such a deep sleep.

I thanked God for the visit I so badly needed. Since then, in other dreams, I've asked Him to take me up again, but He hasn't. I can't wait to go home. That experience was amazing.

**Ecclesiastes 12:6-7**

6Remember your Creator before the silver cord is loosed, Or the golden bowl is broken, Or the pitcher shattered at the fountain,

Or the wheel broken at the well. 7Then the dust will return to the earth as it was, And the spirit will return to God who gave it.

## 2 Kings 6:17

And Elisha prayed, and said, "LORD. I pray, open his eyes that he may see." Then the LORD opened the eyes of the young man, and he saw. And behold, the mountains was full of horses and chariots of fire all around Elisha.

# This Book

One morning, I was driving my kids to church when the Lord said the craziest thing to me: "Write a book."

Brittany was in the front seat next to me, so I tried to keep this whole conversation in my head. I already freak her out on most days as it is. My first reaction to God was, *You have to be joking.* I only read the Bible. I'm not a "book person" in any way.

But he kept saying it: *Write a book.*

I said, "God, You know my grades in school. Even if I wanted to, I have no idea how or where even to start. English class was not fun for me."

Then he told me what the book would be about. He showed me how life and Scripture are woven together—that you can't have one without the other. I told Him again, "That sounds beautiful, but I don't know how to write a book."

Right then, He showed me a vision of the book cover in my mind: a black background with two hands facing each other, fingers interlocked, light shining through some of the gaps between them.

In that moment, I knew exactly what He wanted: a book about life—a book about how, even in the darkest moments, you can find Him. That's where you go when you don't know where to turn. He's not absent in the darkness. Life and Scripture are tied together. The light between the gaps is Him; even when we can't feel Him, He's there. We are His Word—His Word formed us into reality.

It sounded like a fantastic book, but I still didn't know how to write it.

After that, He stopped explaining the content and gave me only one thing: a name. When I kept telling Him, "I can't," He answered, "Ashley will help you."

That was it. Every time I thought, *I can't,* all I heard back was, *Ashley will help you.* Over and over on the way to church, all I got was: "Ashley, Ashley, Ashley."

I go to a big church with multiple Ashleys, but I knew exactly which one He meant. I remember saying, "God, I barely know her. I've only talked to her in passing—'Hi, hi, how are you?' That's all I really know—and you want me to tell her that she's going to help me write a book because you said she would?"

He just said, "Ashley."

By this point, Brittany was staring me down. She said, "Wait, what? You have your thinking face on." I just said, "Nothing." How was I supposed to explain what was going on in my head when I was still trying to understand it myself?

That day I was scheduled to be in Ryan's room at church, so when we arrived, I walked straight back to class. I got Ryan settled, stood by the door, and then I saw Ashley walk by, which never happens. I thought, *Fine, Lord.*

I asked Brittany to go get her because I couldn't leave the class. I was fully expecting to tell her my story and hear, "Well, you just need to pray about it and make sure," like I usually do.

Instead, Ashley came over, and I began sharing about my drive to church that morning. I usually freak people out when I start talking about my experiences with God, but as I spoke, I noticed she was smiling and getting excited.

When I finished, she said, "I had the same conversation with Him one day."

"You did?" I asked.

"Yes," she said, "He told me to write a book. I told Him no—and well, that was five books ago."

God was right—Ashley helped me. She was so kind, and I deeply appreciated her help, because when I say I was lost, I truly was.

God told me to write this book about a week after a tent revival in Potosi, MO, where my good friend Caleb had prayed for me to have a new boldness. I would need that boldness to put all my "mail" out there for everyone to read. You can't just delete a book once it's out. Without that boldness, this book would never have been written.

Back in March, I went to the Arise Nights service in Springfield, MO, that I mentioned earlier. It's funny how God works. A lady named Ashlee—another Ashley—prayed for me at the altar. She started praying, then paused and said, "I don't know what this means, but I see words coming out of your stomach, like the Word of God."

At the time, I had no idea what she was talking about. Now I understand she was seeing this book.

When the Lord first spoke to me about this book, I knew the main word was "*Reconstruction*." I also saw another name beneath it, but I couldn't quite make it out. I'm almost finished with this book now, and just yesterday I finally understood: *Reconstruction* is the name of the series. There will be many books to follow.

Why me? I have no idea. I remember telling Ashley, "This is the weakest part of my life." She just smiled and said, "That's why He picked you."

This is His book. She was right.

Writing this book has been incredible. From the moment I picked up the pen until I put it down, I've felt pure joy. I didn't even have to think about what to write—there was always another sentence waiting for me before I finished the one I was on.

This book is meant to be a blueprint for others. I encourage you to take a piece of paper and a pen, write down an experience you can't seem to get past, ask God to show you your personal Scripture for it, and look for the light in the darkness.

God is good, and He saved my house, just like He said He would.

**Jeremiah 30:2**

" Thus speaks the LORD God of Israel, saying: 'Write in a book for yourself all the words that I have spoken to you.

www.ingramcontent.com/pod-product-compliance
Lightning Source LLC
Chambersburg PA
CBHW052123090426
42741CB00009B/1923